I'M COMING OUT!

A Story of Triumph Over
Sickness, Dis-ease and Abuse

Lakisha Foxworth

ISBN 978-0-9845161-0-0
Library of Congress Catalog Number 2010924889

Published by
Protective Hands Communications
Riviera Beach, FL
Toll free: 866-457-1203
www.protectivehands.com
Email: info@protectivehands.com

Printed in the United States of America

This book is dedicated with love in honor of my mom, Cynthia L. Johnson.

Table of Contents

Special Thank you

A special thank you to my God and Father, the Lord and Creator of all things. Before I was formed in my mother's womb you knew me and ordained me for such a time as this. The days of my life were recorded in your book. You had my whole life from beginning to end planned out and for that I thank you. I realize that your plans for my life are better than any I could ever conjure up. I love you and I appreciate you Jesus. For all the times I wavered in faith about your plans for my life I apologize. Thank you for not giving up on me.

To my brothers Lenorris and Willie, thank you for loving me unconditionally.

To my spiritual leader, Pastor Phyllis Brandon of Souls Harbor Church, I cannot find words to express my gratitude for you setting the example of a Godly woman for me. I have gained so much knowledge from sitting under your God appointed ministry. I love you Pastor. Thank you for all of your prayers, encouragement and moral support.

To my cousin, Debra and Aunt Dorothy for

believing in me, I thank you. I thank God for all your prayers and encouragement which meant so much at a time I needed motherly love. I am happy to have both of you in my corner.

Thank you Steve White, my editor and publisher for helping me to realize my dream and for allowing God to have His way!

Thank you to all my brothers and sisters in Christ. Your love and prayers have kept me going when I would have fallen. You were there with a smile, a hug, words of encouragement and prayer. As the songwriter penned "I Need You To Survive." That is a lesson I've learned through this process. May God continue to bless you and make his face shine upon you always.

Introduction

So many people are struggling with pain and sickness and they need encouragement, an example of someone making it.

It is not God's will that any of His children should perish, but that we should repent and all inherit eternal life. While on this earth, God desires to see you blessed, healthy, strong and joyful.

I am writing this book to present myself as an example of how to survive and triumph over abuse, disappointments and sickness. My desire is to inspire you to live and not die and to develop an intimate relationship with Jesus Christ. I bear witness that He can be your best friend, your healer and your keeper if you'll let Him.

Please read and enjoy my story of triumph through faith and the love of God. May God bless and keep you.

CHAPTER ONE

Our Little Miracle

While in middle school, my mom became pregnant with my younger brother. She was working a full-time job at the time and shortly after we became aware of her pregnancy, she became ill. Mom had to stop working and she was put on complete bed rest. My older brother and I had to assume the responsibility of running the house.

I was going on thirteen at the time and my brother was sixteen. My brother did the driving and together we did the grocery shopping, cooked the meals and of course, we looked after our mom.

One constant in our lives, was an older woman who often came by to check on our mother. Whenever she visited, she would always tie my mother's belly because, according to the elderly woman, this would hold my little brother in and keep him from coming early.

Because of the complications my mother

was experiencing with her pregnancy her doctors had given her a very bleak diagnosis. It was suggested that she consider aborting the baby, but this was totally against my mother's beliefs and her deep faith in God. She told the doctors to do their part and God would surely do His. Indeed He did.

However I don't want to minimize the challenges my mother faced with her pregnancy. The reality is that my mother had severe complications. She hemorrhaged for two and a half months and she ended up delivering my brother after only five months of pregnancy.

My little brother was born on December 23, 1987 weighing one pound and five ounces. Because of the many complications of a premature birth, my brother spent nearly five months in the hospital on various machines and he endured numerous surgeries. Finally, we were able to bring our little *miracle* home. He required monitors both day and night and he also required the services of a nurse to look after him during the day while our mother worked.

Life has not been easy for my little brother. He has been in special education classes since pre-K. He was diagnosed with Attention Deficit Hyperactivity Disorder (ADHD) and other learning disabilities. It has been a struggle for him. My brother has dealt with his personal challenges while also watching our mother battle her illness.

When he was in elementary school, our mom went through several medical procedures, including heart bypass surgery. It was a scary time for the entire family. However as a family we all continued to move forward.

In middle school, my brother did fairly well, making the honor roll several times, but the illness that our mother faced continued. When my brother was in the sixth grade, our mother had another major surgery and she never returned home except to visit for a couple of days during the year. She was eventually placed in a local nursing home. As the big sister, I took on the responsibility of caring for my younger brother.

We visited our mom often when she was in the hospital and we continued to visit her as often as possible when she was in the nursing home. I tried to shield my brother from as much as possible because I didn't want him consumed with worry. He was unable to fully comprehend what was going on and sometimes I thought that was good.

With our mother in the hospital and then a nursing home, our days became fairly routine. After putting my brother on the bus each morning, I would go to the hospital, but I always got home in time to greet my brother when he returned from school.

I would prepare his dinner and afterwards, I would take him to visit our mother. Sometimes, the routine would be interrupted because our mother had to undergo another surgery. Those were the times when dinner would come later or we would eat from the hospital cafeteria.

There were other times when my brother would stay with our neighbors or family members while I visited the hospital and did what I could for our mom. This was our life throughout his middle school years.

At the end of his eighth grade year, our mom was doing better. Previously, she had a partial leg amputation and she was scheduled to have an additional portion of her leg removed. The doctors gave us reason to be-

4

lieve that following surgery, Mom would come home. We began preparing for her arrival. Among other things, we made the house wheelchair accessible.

Although she did not come home, she was able to make it to my brother's graduation ceremony. He was so proud and happy to have our mother there, even though she was in a wheelchair. He couldn't stop smiling. Afterwards, mom and I went out to lunch.

The next week I had a graduation party for him with all the trimmings and all the family came. Little did I know God was pushing me to have this party for a reason. At one point, my mom asked me why I was going all out for the party and I really didn't have an answer. I just had a strong feeling from within to get the family together for this gathering. It was great and my brother was so happy to have our mom there.

My mom told me how proud she was of me. I was excited to show her all of the accommodations we made to get ready for her arrival. I had the cabinets arranged so that everything was reachable from her wheelchair. With Medicaid approval, we were able to order a motorized scooter for my mother and the City in which we lived agreed to build a wheelchair ramp so that our mother would have easy access in and out of the house. I also contacted Hospice for their caregiver support and they agreed to come and do an assessment to make sure that we were properly prepared for our mother's arrival.

I really felt that we were finally going to get our life back to a somewhat normal situation. It was going to be nice to have our mother in the house with me and my little brother. Up until this point, I had been afraid to be in the house by myself. However, when placed in certain situations, you find supernatural strength to do things you don't think you are ready to handle. My mom's declining health motivated me to handle things I didn't think I was capable of handling.

Although we made all of the necessary preparations for our mother to join us for what we hoped would be a long time, less than two weeks later our mother passed away.

After successfully completing middle school and while still dealing with our mother's passing, my brother went on to high school where he was enrolled in a special program designed to prepare exceptional students for life after school. They taught skills such as how to do laundry, personal hygiene, and how to recognize signs in the public. Everything was designed to make him as independent as possible.

During his senior year in high school, he competed in the Special Olympics state competition for track and he attended the senior prom. To see him in his tuxedo, escorting his date to the prom and to dinner was a wonderful experience for the both of us.

It has always been very important to me that he has the experiences of typical teenagers. He sees himself as a regular teen with the same desires. He wants to drive his own car, have his own place, and get married. You name it, he desires it. I try my best to encourage him. I don't want to discourage any of his dreams.

Today, my miracle brother is a high school graduate. He stands five feet three inches and weighs about one hundred seventeen pounds. Not bad for someone who came into this world weighing one pound and five ounces. In addition to graduating from high school, my brother has also completed a year of community college.

Our local community college had a pilot program that accepted students with disabilities. The program was aimed at giving the students a certain level of independence by teaching them how to ride the city bus, manage their money, various job training skills and job placement. Only twelve students throughout the county were chosen for the program. The selection process was highly competitive, but with God's grace, my brother was selected to attend. He learned great job skills through the program and he has benefited tremendously. My brother is a pistol to say the least and I love him very much.

Nightmare (Mom's struggle)

When I was growing up, no one was a stronger example of faith than my mother. We never had much as far as material things, but my mother gave all she had for her children and she modeled faith in God. I was truly blessed to watch her believe in the impossible and receive from God what she believed for. God gifted my mom with the ability to see into the future different events that were going to take place and she had keen discernment. She knew God had a work for me to do and she sacrificed her life for mine. My mom loved everybody and no matter how they treated her, she was good to them. I learned from her that you don't do evil for evil but you let God fight your battles. In the last years of her life, God showed himself strong and mighty in the midst of horrendous suffering.

€

Eight months or more and still counting; this is how long our nightmare has been and it doesn't seem to want to end. My mother went in for gastric bypass surgery on December 29, 2000. The doctor stated it was medically necessary to improve her quality of life. At the time, she was on oxygen, a sleep apnea machine and struggled with COPD (chronic obstruction pulmonary disease) along with high blood pressure. We were told it was a successful surgery; she was discharged on January 8, 2001. Over the next couple weeks it became apparent that the surgery wasn't as successful as we had been led to believe. My mother constantly struggled to keep her food and medicines down with little to no avail.

About three weeks after my mother's release from the hospital her situation was no better.

After having sharp pains in her left leg for a couple of days she then had an excruciating pain in her right leg that almost crippled her and scared her so bad that she called 911 herself. My thirteen year old brother was too upset to make the call. She was screaming to the top of her lungs because of the pain.

I remember it was about five thirty in the afternoon and I was turning the corner of our street coming home from work. There were several ambulances with flashing lights all over our yard and driveway. I got nervous because I had no idea what was going on. I spotted my little brother running up and down the sidewalk scared, shaking and yelling because he didn't know what to do. I don't remember putting the car in park, but I guess I did. I hopped out and ran to my little brother, hugged and comforted him. I let him know that it was going to be alright, and then I ran into the house. The rescue workers tried to prevent me from coming inside, but I quickly let them know that I lived here and the person they were treating was *my* mother.

I ran in to hear my mom shrilling from the pain. I was shook up and confused. I didn't know what was going on but to hear her voice let me know she was still alive and that gave me a little relief. They were trying to remove my mom from the back bedroom and get her into the ambulance, but her severe pain and screams made even the paramedics nervous.

Finally, they placed my mother in the ambulance and rushed her to the hospital's emergency room which was up the street from our house. Immediately the doctors tried various pain medications but none of them were able to take the edge off the pain.

The surgeon who had performed the gastric bypass was called in and he insisted on emergency surgery. He said it was the only way to relieve the pain. He believed it was a blood clot that had formed and he said it could possibly move up to a major organ and kill her. This was a tough pill to swallow because it was so sudden. We reluctantly agreed to the surgery which took about an hour and a half.

First, the doctor did exploratory surgery, examining both of my mother's legs. He discovered a clot in her right leg and removed it. Afterwards, he told us it was a good idea to do the surgery. He stated that the left leg didn't look good either, but because of the late hour he didn't see a need to bother it.

Mom spent the next couple of days in the Critical Care Unit where they maintained a close watch of her legs. The nurses kept her legs covered with socks and blankets and sometimes, even heaters. They would use a board to elevate her legs to increase the circulation of her blood. The doctor would come by with his *Doppler* test to check for pulses. We watched and prayed, hoping for the best.

Everyday, I made it a point to be there when the doctor came in to hear the report and see where we were headed. Over time, my mother had two more surgeries to correct her problems. They cut her in the groin area on both sides of her legs, doing a skin graft, and cutting up and down both sides of her legs from top to bottom. This was to no avail because eventually the left leg turned dark due to poor circulation.

My mother's room was at the end of the hall because of her constant cries of pain. One night, the doctor came to visit her and he informed us that something was very wrong. There was no pulse in her left leg and it was very cool to the touch. He stated that something drastic had to be done or else my mom could lose her life due to *sepsis*, which is a condition where toxins form in the tissue or bloodstream.

The medical terminology I didn't understand, but I did understand when the doctor said that the solution was to amputate her leg. This was a shock and we had to make a decision on the spot. It was a life or death situation, we were told. My mom had to sign the forms authorizing the surgery. She grudgingly agreed, while hoping for a miracle.

The next day, which was a Saturday, I went to the hospital to comfort and support my mom as they prepared her for her fourth surgery. Her left leg was amputated due to infection and the fear of sepsis.

During this time mom was in excruciating pain and there was really no pain medicine that totally relieved her. She began hallucinating from all the medicines and she could be heard all day and night crying from pain. It was really unbearable. The pain was tortuous for my mother and it was very hard for us to see our mother in such agony and we were unable to do anything about it. I had to call on Jesus constantly to maintain sanity and to stay strong for my mother.

A week later mom's right leg started acting up, her breathing became rapid, and she was depressed, she wasn't at all herself.

One Sunday morning I went by the hospital before going to church to check on my mom. I could barely pull myself away because my mother's breathing was very fast and uneven. She was on a regular floor, which meant her nurse had several other patients to look after and could not give her one on one attention.

What I witnessed shook me up so that I reported it to her nurse who in turn called her doctor. The nurse assured me mom would be okay, so I decided to go to church. When I returned to the hospital after church, the nurse informed me that my mother had gone into respiratory failure. She was immediately transferred to the Critical Care Unit and within minutes, they put her on a ventilator. This was not enough to calm her down; she fought it, acting out from agitation. They sedated her using a combination of drugs and chemically paralyzed her so she couldn't move.

The family had gathered in a room and we were told that she might not make it through the night. I did not want to hear this nor could I accept the possibility that my mother would pass away. My best friend at the time drove me to church because prayer meeting was about to begin. She drove fast to get me there. I made it out of the car and rushed in where I shared the news with my pastor and her husband. We gathered in a tight circle. I laid my head on her shoulder while they prayed. I cried and prayed with them. My mother made it through the night.

During the week numerous blood tests and cultures were done and her white blood cell count was rising. This meant infection had set in and her electrolytes were off which signaled problems with her kidneys.

Seeing my mom laid up in the hospital bed, unable to move and hooked up to so many machines was very difficult, but it's weird how I never thought this was the end of her life. I just always felt like somehow we were going to get through this.

We were all trying to hold off on doing anymore surgery, but by the end of the week, it was a life or death situation. Something drastic had to be done. This meant her right leg had to be amputated. We were told this was the only way to give her a chance to make it. I had to sign authorizing the surgery, all the while not sure if I was doing the right thing.

With my mom in a state of unconsciousness, hooked up to a ventilator and various IV tubes, they wheeled her into surgery to remove a part of her right leg. This was my mother's fifth major surgery since being admitted to the hospital in January. However, this was her fourteenth trip to OR. There was the gastric bypass in December and in between her major surgeries, she went down every other day for deep cleaning of the remaining portion of her left leg. This was a very extensive procedure requiring anesthesia. So in essence it amounted to another surgical procedure.

Through God's grace and mercy she made it. She spent approximately three months on life support. It was such a victory when they were able to reduce her dependence on the life support machines. But ultimately there would be setbacks and her dependence on the machines would increase.

Some said she would never come off the life support machines, but I refused to accept that.

I would read scripture in her ear and leave gospel music playing near her head in my absence. By mid-February I stopped working to see after my mom and my baby brother. I spent my days and nights at the hospital. Occasionally, I worked half-days as a substitute teacher. But on my breaks I was calling the hospital because it was so hard for me to leave my mother alone.

My mother had more surgeries which included a feeding tube being placed in her abdomen and a trachea in her throat. She also had a Hickman catheter inserted because all of her veins had been exhausted. I counted each successful procedure a blessing because they were helping to keep my mother alive. It was tough but with each successful surgery, I felt that we were on our way.

There were still close calls here and there. I remember one time mom started bleeding and the doctors didn't know where the blood was coming from and this was thought to be life threatening. The doctors didn't give her too long to live if the source of the bleeding couldn't be found soon and stopped successfully.

After I received the negative report from the nurse, I left the hospital and ran to my church.

It was the middle of the day around lunch time. I found my pastor's husband there and I fell to my knees basically begging for help and crying. He called my pastor on the speaker phone and we all prayed together. By nightfall, the bleeding had subsided and the forecast was better. Thank you Jesus was all I could say.

Mom eventually made it out of the Critical Care Unit after spending a little over four months there. She spent another couple months in the hospital itself and she went through many more deep cleaning procedures.

My mom was discharged one day in July to a nursing home and re-admitted to the hospital the next day because she had problems keeping her medication and food down. She couldn't even keep water down. She spent the next 11 days in the hospital where they took pictures and x-rays and gave her IV nutrition.

Again, without the problem being resolved, she was discharged to a second nursing home about twenty-five miles from our home. She spent five days there and it was back to the hospital with the same problem. She wasn't able to keep her food/drink or medicine down. She was dehydrated. This time she spent a week in the hospital and numerous diagnostic tests were performed.

They found the problem to be a high grade narrowing in the region where her food and liquid intake is supposed to pass through. A gastroenterologist attempted to dilate it with a balloon and endoscope but it was too complex. He felt more advance equipment was needed. Her primary doctor arranged to have her sent to a different hospital. After all the paperwork was done and transport was ready, his office called and cancelled the orders. Her admitting doctor refused to get her the care she needed, so she remained in the same hospital for two more weeks.

No moves were scheduled; no specific course of action or treatment took place. This was so frustrating and sad. I traveled back and forth every day, sometimes more than once to see after my mom. We went back and forth trying to get her the care she needed. The result was to release her to another nursing home with the promise that from there she would be seen by her primary physician who was on call at the nursing home. He was going to see to it that she got the care she needed. She was at the

19

nursing home for nine days. She didn't see a doctor, no plan of action taken and she still had problems holding food, drink and medicine down.

I would call her primary doctor's office only to be told that during the time my mother was in the nursing home, he was not her doctor. At the same time the nurses were telling me that her primary doctor was indeed her doctor and he was aware of her condition. He had even prescribed medication for her, according to the nurses. I had to threaten to call the news media to get him to finally come out and see her. I felt like everyone was just sitting around waiting on my mom to waste away. The doctor's response was to send my mother to another hospital.

She had a couple of procedures done at this hospital and spent a week or so there and then she was sent to another nursing home just a few miles from our home. She spent the next six to nine months there before she passed away.

CHAPTER TWO

Growing Up Too Soon

When I was fourteen I convinced my mother to help me get a part-time job at a local fast food restaurant working nights and weekends. Although I was only fourteen, I was very physically developed and therefore I looked older than I was. However, my appearance somewhat betrayed me, because I was very naïve and innocent.

One late night after work, I accepted a ride home from an older guy who was a regular customer at the restaurant. He was twenty-two and I was fifteen at the time. Accepting the ride proved to be one of the biggest mistakes of my life. A man that I had come to trust and someone that I thought I knew because he was a familiar face betrayed me and violated my trust. I was raped and my innocence was shattered.

I remember looking up towards the sky, asking God why this was happening to me. What had I done to deserve this? I honestly thought I was dying. I guess you could say a part of me did die that day, figuratively speaking.

Sadly, I lacked knowledge when it came to interacting with the opposite sex and that made me somewhat vulnerable. The bible states in Hosea 4:6 that *"My people perish for the lack of knowledge."* And because of my innocence and lack of experience in dealing with boys and men, I was without knowledge.

Looking back, I also realize that my self-esteem was very low at the time. So when guys, many of them older than me, flirted and came on to me, I just smiled nervously. I was very scared to let anyone close to me so most of the time it ended with seemingly harmless flirting.

The man that raped me was able to penetrate my wall of defense using shrewd manipulation. He befriended me by coming into the restaurant frequently and talking to me about school and about people that we both knew. As a matter of fact, I went to school with one of his relatives.

I began to trust him and I even had a couple of phone conversations with him. He never came off as a mean person and he certainly didn't seem to have any ulterior motives. His appearance was also non-threatening. He was a soft spoken man that wore wiry glasses. Unlike most of the other men that came into the restaurant, he never said anything out of the way that would arouse my suspicions. In many ways I was a victim of my innocence and my lack of self-esteem.

Because of my experiences as a child and young lady, as a woman I have chosen to make the teaching of abstinence to young girls the focus of much of my work. I want to equip young girls with the necessary skills and the confidence to say "no" to unwanted sexual advances. It's important to me that young girls recognize when older guys are trying to manipulate them and take advantage of their naiveté. No matter what, a girl has to remember an older guy has more life experiences than she does. I also want young girls to love themselves and realize their value.

Often, girls give in to having sex or accept being mistreated just for the attention or because they fear being alone. However, if young girls recognized their worth, they would not be vulnerable and certain behavior would not be acceptable. They would demand the respect they are worthy of.

I am in a good place in my life now with a meaningful and rewarding job, but my journey from a rape survivor to a woman teaching abstinence and helping young girls build their self-esteem was not an easy journey. As you will read there have been many other challenges along the way. I have faced challenges that I could have never imagined and yet through God's grace I have survived and actually triumphed.

CHAPTER THREE

Sex Is Not A Game

An Open Letter to Teens

Sex is not a game, and it's not something to do just because you feel like it or because everyone else is doing it or your boy/girlfriend wants you to. When making the decision to lay down with someone you need to count up the cost and realize you may be doing something enjoyable for a moment but painful for a lifetime. It could very well cost you your life.

As an infant, I was molested and because of it I grew up being afraid of people in general and men in particular. Because of what happened to me as an infant, I am still amazed at the fact that I have been able to be with a man. See, my sexual violations didn't stop in my infancy, as a teenager, I was raped twice and molested by a family friend. Finally, I just gave in to having sex.

The second time I was raped it was by a guy I had willingly engaged in sex with before. I happened to meet him at my first job as well. One evening he came through my *drive thru* window and flirted with me. I felt special to have gained his attention. He gave me his phone number and told me to call him and then out of nowhere, he kissed me. Afterwards, we talked on the phone and he would come visit me on my breaks at work.

Let me tell you ladies, he was all that. I was young and immature and I had this thing like most females my age. I was attracted to him because he was a red bone, thick and muscular, *"good"* hair, big, beautiful lips, and he could really dress. So when I, with low self-esteem and no schooling on the opposite sex was approached by this older, fine brother, I was putty in his hands. He gave me special attention, which I longed for and I thought he could make me forget my past and what I was going through at home. He was the first guy I ever gave myself to.

Girls and parents listen, he gave me attention. For example, he paid me compliments on my hair, my face, my clothes, my voice, etc. He talked about things that mattered to me, things no one else cared to discuss. I was most impor-

tant in his world whenever we were together.

This man was filling a void in my life. That's why it's vital for parents to talk to their kids and give them quality time instead of concerning themselves with bills and work. If you don't give it to them someone else will.

One evening I was at a party drinking, being fast with my friends and he came up whispering in my ear, kissing on me and I left with him, one of my friends and his cousin. We went back to his apartment. He wanted to have sex and I was all right with that until he refused to wear a condom.

This time he just wasn't himself; he was very mean and different, not sweet and careful like before. I never had to ask him to use protection before; it was something he took care of without fail. He adamantly refused this night and I tried to leave but he wouldn't let me. He forced me down and raped me. I begged and pleaded for him to at least use protection but he wouldn't let up no matter how hard I fought. During the act, I felt like something was very wrong but I couldn't put my finger on it. Afterwards, I went to the doctor to get checked and all was well, so I thought.

27

I didn't see the guy for two to three years and even then it was from afar. But I did take notice of the fact that he had lost a lot of weight. I questioned God as to why he wouldn't let me see the guy again, just let me run into him, I thought. But God was protecting me, I know that now.

Years later, while home on break, I learned that he had died. I got a phone call from a friend asking if I'd heard about his death. After the call ended, I dropped to my knees and cried out to God. I prayed his soul was in heaven and that he had gotten things right with God before leaving this earth. I told God I had forgiven him and not to hold anything against him and to please spare him.

I remember my mom was at work and I was in her bedroom praying and crying before the Lord and reading Jeremiah 29.11. When my mom came home she was in an unusually good mood. She cooked my favorite meal of salmon croquettes, grits and pork & beans.

According to my mother, the reason she was cooking my favorite meal was due to the fact that the Lord spoke to her on her way home from work and told her to do it. He didn't tell her why but He had her stop at the store to pick up the ingredients. I was comforted that night by my special meal and being with my mom. I still hadn't told her anything I was going through. She didn't pressure me for answers, but she looked at me strange and said it was the weirdest thing for God to tell her to do this tonight for Kisha.

CHAPTER FOUR

My Discovery

I had graduated high school and gone away to college. During my first year in college I kept hearing rumors from back home that the guy was infected. So when I went to the clinic on campus for my regular check up, I asked to get checked for all STDS to dispel any rumors and eliminate my concerns. I remember the nurse asking me how often I used condoms while having sex. I said ninety-five percent of the time and she said, "Only ninety-five percent of the time?" I didn't like her comment but I blew it off.

A couple weeks went by and I got a call from the clinic to come in for my results. I went in, thinking it was no big deal. I was ready to hear all was well when they showed me to the doctor's office. He was waiting with a lady. They asked me to have a seat. The doctor said he had good news and bad news and asked which would I like to hear first? I said the good, of course. He said well you don't have syphilis, gonorrhea, Chlamydia, or herpes. I was so relieved that I didn't even think about what the bad news could be. He said the bad news is you tested positive for HIV.

My life changed that day. Here I was 18 years old with a life sentence. I was in prison. He didn't look sick when I was with him, I thought to myself, but what I didn't know was HIV doesn't have a certain look and my man had been with at least 100 girls, if not more because he had it like that.

So you can understand why I really want young people to understand that it *can* happen to them. They are not invincible. When people tell you not to have sex until marriage it's not to take away your fun, it's to protect you, to keep you safe and possibly save your life.

Please don't find yourself like me, scared and lonely and regretting that I didn't wait until I was married. Sex is great but it is not worth your life.

€

I was a freshman in college, just beginning to experience college life and looking forward to the future. When I was given the results and told that I was HIV positive, everything from that moment on was like a bad dream.

I walked back to my dorm in a fog. Everything was a blur and I felt numb. I wanted to wake up from this bad dream and go on preparing to enjoy the holidays with my family like all the other students. Along the way, I stopped by the campus post office out of habit and immediately ran into a girl I knew from home. She spoke to me and I spoke to her, but mentally I was not all there and I just kept walking. When I reached my room, I closed the door, and dropped to my knees. I cried and asked God, why me? For some reason, I didn't dwell there very long. I prayed and told God that I knew he was able to heal me, to help me. Beginning that very day, I was determined to fight for my life and I did.

I had already begun attending church regularly, but I became more committed and dedicated. I attended prayer service daily. I read the Word of God, morning, noon and night. I even forsook my school work because nothing else mattered. I remember many times feeling as though this was it and the end was here. I would lie down not knowing if I would ever rise again.

One morning there was an elderly cleaning lady vacuuming outside my dorm room. Most of the students were in class, but I was lying on my bed, racked in pain, tormented in my mind and crying out to God. For some reason, one of us opened the door and she looked at me. I was ashamed because of the way I looked. I spoke and quickly closed the door. But that was not the last I would see of her.

A little while later, she knocked on my door and told me to read Psalm 25. I was comforted that day by the words of that particular Psalms. I dissected it and applied it to my life. God had used the cleaning lady to make a difference in my life. I was encouraged to run on.

I also spent lots of money calling home to talk with my mom, often unsure if it would be our last conversation, but I never let on. I put a lot of miles on my car going home at least once a month to see my mom and little brother.

One lesson I learned is that you can't judge a person based on their outer appearance be-cause a person can be smiling outwardly and frowning inwardly. I put up a good front. I was crippled with fear, shame, regret, guilt, and pride. I wanted to run away and disappear. Like my brother Job in the Bible, I felt like cursing the day I was born.

While in college, there was an evangelist that spoke a word directly to me during service. She told me the Lord had given her a message. According to her the Lord said, "He's doing it because He can. He is God and He doesn't have to ask anyone's permission. He does what He wants to do."

I was blessed, because now I was certain I would be healed. I had been questioning why God chose to bless me and heal me. I was also unsure of how to answer those who might ask me questions and I was concerned about how they would respond to me if I answered them honestly.

It is only now that I realize the majority of my battle was in my mind. The mind is the place where you decide to accept or reject thoughts and conditions. For years, I chose to accept lies. I feared being rejected by people, which has happened to me as it has probably happened to you. However, I now know that someone's rejection is not the end of the world. What is important is that God, the Creator

Himself, accepted me just as I was. I was a filthy mess, dying and on my way to hell. Yet, He saw that I was fit for use and for that I am eternally grateful.

After my initial diagnosis, I spent all my time in the word of God because I felt safe and comforted and close to Him while reading His word. It's a lifeline to me. When I wasn't reading I was praying and fasting often. There were times where at the drop of a hat, I would fall to my knees and pray. At those times, I felt peace and comfort for my weary soul. I also was comforted by Psalms 91 and 139. The Psalms encouraged me that God was my protector and He understood me. I would recite scripture constantly including "Greater is He that is within me, than he that is in the world" (1 John 4:4).

This was a weapon when the pain and struggle of life got overwhelming and seemed to go out of control. I just totally shut myself off from the rest of the world, including school and my finances. I had received a few thousand dollars from grants and loans. That was big money to me but it didn't matter. I would just give it away to beggars on the streets. I thought in a way that this act would help me as well, giving to those in need. Money didn't matter; it was such a little thing when your life seemed to be slipping away.

During this time, my mom was working for a wealthy family. I realized as much as this family liked us and would do anything to help us; I was dealing with something money couldn't solve. I realized how limited we are as human beings and how much we need God in our lives. I realized that there were issues that money or a super duper mom couldn't fix.

My mom was awesome. She sacrificed her life for her children, but not even she could save me. As a child there wasn't a problem in the world that my mother couldn't fix. But now I had encountered a problem that even she couldn't get me out of. How I longed for her to sweep in and save me and make it all better. I even wished that she could punish me as if I was a child. I would have taken a beaten any day over this.

Ultimately, I had to accept that this was a problem that would not easily disappear. So I spent my college career sneaking, ducking and hiding so that people would not find out my secret.

When I first found out about my HIV positive diagnosis, I made note of everyone I had wronged in any way. I went down the list calling to apologize, trying to get my life in order. I somehow felt that I was being punished and I thought this act would change things. The enemy had such a strong hold on my mind.

I was so concerned about others discovering my secret that I was careful to go to a doctor whose office was on the outskirts of the city. I would look around to make sure no one was following me before getting out of the car to go into the office. While there, I was a nervous wreck. Whenever the door opened, I would look up, hoping and praying that no one I knew was coming in. I also hoped that no one working in the doctor's office knew me. In other words, I was always looking over my shoulder. Every three months when I visited the lab to get my blood drawn, I found myself still looking over my shoulder.

This made for a difficult, unpleasant existence. The ironic thing is that I could actually forget about my circumstances when I didn't have an appointment with the doctor, meaning that I had no tests to take or during the time when I didn't have any pills to swallow.

With God's help, I could go to class, work and hang out with friends for periods of time as if everything was normal. Then I would go home, take my medicine and go to bed. My secret lived with me, but God's grace was sufficient to sustain me.

In college, I can remember one particular day when I must have been getting used to some new medications because I was sick to the stomach to the point where I could barely tear myself away from the bathroom. I was trying to get to a theatre class and I was trying to avoid embarrassment. I went to class but I had to leave out. To save face, I ran half way across campus to use a secluded restroom even though I was sick. With little relief, I hiked back across campus to catch the end of the class. These were crazy times. No one knew what was going on except God. He was and still is my best friend. I felt as though I couldn't tell anyone because they wouldn't understand.

€

In nineteen ninety-five, I had become good friends with an old roommate who had brought me to the Lord after prodding me to go to church. I felt a special connection to her. When I gave my life to Christ she rejoiced. I was so eager to learn, I bombarded her with questions constantly. We were both from South Florida and when we came home on break I visited her often and even spent the night at her home a few times.

On one occasion, we were speaking about Jesus and I opened up to her. I shared my diagnosis. It was the first time I had shared this information with anyone. She let me know that my revelation didn't change our relationship. She made it clear that I was the same girl she had always known and I was her friend. "You're a living testimony," she said. I can't explain how good it felt to be accepted.

I remember spending the night with her and going to an "old school" church in a little town where they used washboards and the wooden floor to make music. Oh, what a time we had. They sung a song that said, "Jesus can fix it." I remember thinking, "God I believe the words to that song, fix it for me Jesus."

In spite of the wonderful church services, that was a tough weekend that I spent with my friend. I was in so much pain. I ached all over, inside and out. I don't know what was going on, I just hurt. At times, I felt like my heart would jump out of my chest, but I told no one.

When I arrived at my friend's house after church, I got some anointed oil and shut myself up in the bedroom. I prayed and cried out to God and asked Him to take my life, not to let me wake up in the morning. The pain was too much. I anointed myself and I sincerely prayed to God to end my life. I believe God heard me so I was surprised to wake up the next morning. I wasn't excited, but rather perplexed.

Why hadn't God honored my prayer? What was the use of me still living? Obviously God had a plan and ultimately it wasn't about me, it was about God getting the glory out of my life.

Later, while still in college, I told a pastor about my dilemma and he referred me to a scripture in the bible. The scripture was Lamentations 3:22-26. I interpreted the scripture to mean that I should suffer in silence, so I endured my pain without complaining. I now realize that's not really what that scripture means.

On the contrary, as a young person, I can go through storms in preparation for fulfilling my purpose in God. I can lean and depend on God, the only one able to save, heal and deliver me, man can't do it.

Over time, I learned how to thank God through pain and disappointment. At first, I thought it was crazy to say thank you every time a pain hit me, but I did anyway. Eventually, it became a habit. I also learned to work through the pain. Very few people knew what I was going through. I told them of my diagnosis, but I never told them about the pain. I just couldn't find the words.

For two years, I had told no one but Jesus. He is my best friend and I talked to Him daily. Day and night I would walk the halls of my dorm, talking, praying and crying out to the Lord. I could trust Him with my secret. I knew that God wouldn't spread rumors about me or put me down.

I remember looking at my body and noticing the changes, feeling the pain, but not knowing what was going on. The enemy used this against me; he would say things like, "yeah you see those marks and those veins popping out. You see your skin changing." But I fought the negative thoughts.

With my body racked in pain, experiencing

severe bouts of diarrhea and the enemy speaking defeat and death in my ear, I went to classes, worked part-time, interned and ultimately graduated with honors, earning a Bachelor's degree by the grace of God.

I remember walking across the stage both happy and sad. I was happy because of my personal accomplishment and because I was making my family proud. I was sad because I was lonely, bound by sickness, fear and oppression.

By now, I had revealed everything to my mom, but I hid my pain from her. I was basically living a lie. I smiled and laughed at the right times, all the while I was crying inside. There were many times I wanted to cry out loud, just scream and yell what I was dealing with, but I never did.

On a personal note, I had made a vow to God and myself a few months before I found out that I was infected to not have sex again until I was married. I was fed up with feeling used, dirty and empty. I didn't feel loved or respected. I now realize that God was working on me even then. So with this vow and then my diagnosis, I began a private life. I turned within and put up huge walls around me. I would allow people to get only so close and then I would shut them out. I barely dated while completing my undergraduate degree. But then I hardly dated in high school. After my traumatic event at age 15, my mom sheltered me and so my dating experiences were kept to a minimum.

There was a period of time when I was in what may appear to be denial of the whole situation. I had claimed my healing with all my heart and I believed. I convinced myself it was all a lie and that I was healthy like anyone else my age. And because I wasn't having sex I didn't tell anyone I talked to. I was convinced that nothing was there.

€

I remember taking a shower one night in the dorm bathroom that I shared with about twenty girls. I was scrubbing as hard as I could, even using a little bleach trying to get rid of the filthy feeling I had. The spirit of God spoke to me telling me that I cannot clean the inside no matter how hard I scrubbed; only God can clean both inside and out.

I remember one day in prayer at the church, I was on my knees and it was as if someone spoke to me, saying you've prayed and asked long enough, now you must begin to thank Him. Thank God for your healing.

After the revelation, I decided to leave college for a semester. I went home, worked and claimed my healing. I took no medication, I just believed. I grew in grace and my faith increased.

One day I began to lose my hearing which turned out to be tied to a weakened immune system according to the doctor. The doctor decided to test me for HIV and the results came back positive. But remember, I had claimed my healing and walked it out for the past several years, but here it was not yet manifested.

So I had to go to doctors and start taking medication to appease the health professionals and my mom. For several years I did this. I went through bouts of getting used to medications, struggling to keep my faith and continue in school. At times, I was taking 12-16 pills in the morning and then again at night. It was difficult to say the least. There have been medications that I've taken that listed the side effects as possible death. I had to really pray to God and remind myself of His word found in St. Mark, chapter 16:18, *"that if I take of poison it will not hurt me.*" It was God's grace and mercy that kept me. I was scared as I read the labels on the prescription bottles, but I found comfort in the word of God.

Over the years I have had approximately five surgeries to correct my hearing. Thank God for His healing, because I haven't had any problems with my hearing now for nearly three years. I had a friend ask me if I knew how it felt not being able to hear. Yes, most definitely I do.

Several times over my adult life, I have lost hearing in one or both of my ears. I know what it's like to sit in a room full of people and not hear a single word being said, not even by the person sitting next to you. I don't know why God allowed this to happen but I figured it was a way for me to get closer to God and talk to Him because He was the only one who could understand what I was going through. He was with me all the time and I was shut off from the world. I learned to read lips but it was very frustrating to say the least. I even had people make fun of me because they would be sitting right next to me and I wouldn't be able to hear them and they thought it was funny. I laughed too because it seemed ridiculous, however, I was sad inside.

While earning my undergraduate degree, I let only three people in on my secret. God had prompted me to share with these three people otherwise I wouldn't have told them. He knew I needed someone to lean on and I thank Him for His infinite wisdom and sovereignty. I had to face the spirit of death many times and I had to trust God. God had promised me long life. He gave me His word that I was healed and that it would be manifested. I stood on that word and I found strength in Numbers 23:19 which state that *"God is not a man that He should lie nor the son of man that he should repent."*

I had to swallow my pride and get help. I ran into a few people who knew me or knew of me while picking up prescriptions or visiting the doctor. This was not easy because of the stigma, the cruelty and curiosity of people in general. I was embarrassed and afraid of what they might do with the information. I feared rejection; I was just a fearful mess. This totally goes against God's word that says "God has not given us the spirit of fear but of love, power and a sound mind." (2 Timothy 1:7).

I allowed myself to be held in prison, in

bondage in my mind. I have learned that things are never as bad as we make them out to be. We can conjure up a whole lot of mess and be so off the mark it's ridiculous. But God is faithful and just and He forgives us of our sins. (1 John 1:9). Glory to God!

I had to get over myself and realize it is not about me. This thing is so much bigger than me, than anything I could imagine. It's about Jesus, his plan, his glory being revealed. I have not yet arrived. I am still on the potter's wheel and I still need to accept what God is doing in my life. I have to work on it daily. The scriptures will help us remember that we are but clay and we have a great treasure in these earthly vessels. (2 Cor 4:7). Our righteousness is as filthy rags before Him (Isaiah 64:6). We are nothing and can do nothing without Him. Hallelujah!

What kept me going was His word. I always had the Spirit remind me of His promises so when pain was great or I received bad reports from the doctor, I would tell myself, you are not going anywhere until every word God has spoken over your life comes to past. That includes husband, children, ministry, and manifested healing etc. etc. I have lived my life looking forward to what is to come.

When I first decided to leave school about four months after my diagnosis, I had fallen on my knees one day in my dorm room and sincerely cried out to God. I asked Him what I should do. I couldn't continue the way I was going. In my spirit the answer I received was, "go home." I said okay but you're going to have to guide my steps and prepare the way. It was very emotional. People wanted to know why, including my mom. I hadn't shared my secret with her yet so I came up with something. I don't remember what I told her exactly but God smoothed things out.

As I was packing to go home, I was crying and praying to God. I didn't really want to leave, but I felt that this was something I had to do. My friends were awesome and they threw me a surprise going away party and afterwards I was on my way. I took a flight home but the airport where I landed was about 45 minutes away so I caught a train to my town. On that train ride, I encountered something out of this world. I was weak physically so I separated myself from the crowd. I sat in a seat by myself and read my bible. There was an older gentleman across from me who had a terrible cough. He was loud and consistent with it. I turned away from him a little and considered moving. I was weak and did not want to chance getting sick, but I stayed put. I do believe others moved away and kind of shunned him.

For some reason, he talked to me. He was of another race, old and feeble and looked a bit tattered. I was a bit cautious about speaking with him. He asked me what I was reading and he also wanted to know my favorite book in the bible. He shared that he liked the book of Psalms. He told me that he was from the North and that he didn't really have any family left. He said that he was moving to South Florida because of the warm weather. His old body just couldn't take the northern winters anymore.

I was moved with compassion for him. I no longer felt afraid of him but I somehow wanted to help him and take care of him. I had no means to do so but I desired to. I wished him the best and inwardly prayed for him. He just looked in my eyes and said I'm sure we'll see each other again. I prayed for him several times after that when he dropped in my spirit. I believe I entertained an angel unaware. I felt comforted after that encounter.

When I got home, I went directly to my bedroom, dropped to my knees and said okay God I'm here, now what? The answer I received was to go to church, get a job and work.

Within a day of being home, I went to a revival meeting at my home church. I got there a little late so I sat near the back on a crowded pew. The evangelist who was speaking that day was someone I had never heard before. He was ministering to folk. I wasn't there twenty minutes when he called me out.

"Young lady wearing the braids in the back there, will you stand for a moment please?" I looked around to make sure he was speaking to me and then I stood. He said, "You don't know me, never seen me before in your life, is that right?"

"Yes."

"Well God's got his hand on your life. You have been in the hardest struggle of your life," he said.

Suddenly, out of what seemed like nowhere, came a loud cry that stunned me. It was revealed later that the cry came from the pit of my stomach.

The evangelist continued, "You have such a heavy burden on you, something you've shared with no one. God is giving you a miracle; you will never be the same after this night."

He said a couple of other things, but what was profound for me was that God had actually heard all of my prayers. He had been watching and listening and was concerned about me. I had spent months fasting, praying and reading his word, never being one hundred percent sure He was there. But at that moment, He became very real to me and I felt assured that I was on the right track. Oh what a blessing! Hallelujah! God had used one of His servants to encourage me to stay in the race. That man spoke things that I had only uttered to God in secret. I knew without a doubt it was God himself speaking through a vessel.

Shortly thereafter, I was fortunate to get a temporary job with the government making decent money. I also made a commitment to stay in church and maintain my connection to God.

Later, as I began to prepare to return to college, I received a great word from my Pastor. He has since gone on to be with the Lord, but he was well known as a true prophet of God. I loved and respected him very much.

He told me in a service one night that God had given me a green light. It took me quite a few years to understand that word. But the message was for me to go full speed ahead, to run on in the race towards God and everything was going to be alright. Glory to God!

In the Fall I was able to go back to school after spending the summer growing closer to God. However, instead of returning to the dorm and reliving some of the painful memories, I took an off campus apartment with a friend.

I continued to stay off campus while in college except for a semester that I stayed in a scholarship house. I had several roommates and all of them were clueless to my medical diagnosis. I hid it very well. On one occasion, a roommate who had known me since elementary school commented that I seemed distant and had a wall up. She felt as though I didn't want to get too close to people. She was right. I felt as though my card was being pulled and I might be found out but I managed to keep my secret. I was fairly healthy for the most part except for diarrhea from time to time and the hearing loss which went unexplained for quite awhile. I appeared to be like everyone else my age. Looking to get married soon, talking about having kids and attending church regularly. I was blessed to have found a wonderful church home where I could grow and be taught the word of God. God placed me right where I needed to be in order to survive and He had great leaders interceding on my behalf. Only God knows just how much their prayers meant.

I graduated in 1998 and moved back home, not only to care for my mom and younger brother, but also to teach school.

Over the years I have taught at all grade levels for the school district as well as private organizations for special summer programs. In 2002, I began teaching abstinence after my mom passed away and have enjoyed it every since. It's really interesting how I came to teach abstinence.

I was working as a substitute teacher in a middle school while caring for my mom in late 2001 and this particular day the class had a guest speaker. A young lady was teaching abstinence and her lesson for that day was on

HIV/AIDS and other sexually transmitted diseases. I was in awe watching the video and hearing her speak candidly on the issues. I thought to myself how I wished someone had taken the time to teach me such valuable information when I was the age of the students.

I said to myself what an awesome opportunity to share a life saving message and I wanted in. I asked questions about the program and how one might come to work for their organization. Ultimately, I sent my résumé and cover letter and then I waited for their response.

The organization was waiting to see if they were going to be funded through a federal grant. Months later I was contacted and a day after my mom's passing I received a phone call and job offer. Isn't God good! I worked for them for three years and they became family to me. I didn't tell them my secret but they supported me through prayers and words of encouragement. I learned so much about self respect, setting boundaries in relationships, emotional consequences of sex outside of marriage and I'm still learning and sharing what I learn with others.

In 2003, I began dating a guy who talked about marriage from the very beginning of our relationship. He was in the ministry and I fell for him. I prayed and fasted and talked to one of my friends about how badly I wanted to tell him everything about me.

We had been dating for a couple months and I was anxious to tell him right away, but my friend advised me to wait a minute. I didn't really know him or where he came from and I needed to be sure he wouldn't take my story and use it to hurt me in any way. I know others in my situation can understand where I'm coming from. You never quite know when it's the right time to reveal something so personal.

I wanted to be fair to him, but I wanted to get to know him first and be able to trust him. You want to be seen for who you are inside and not for a label. Also I was afraid of being rejected which is why I had rarely dated. But not only did I fear rejection, I was also very shy. Finally, I shared everything with him, all my secrets and he accepted me. I remember how I struggled to tell him. It was the first time in my life I had opened up like that and it caused me to fall deeper for him.

I called him on the phone while he was at work and told him I needed to talk to him about something important. I asked him to come by after work. He tried to get a hint as to what it was but I didn't give him any idea. He later told me that worried him. I was so nervous; I was actually shaking, while holding the phone talking to him. I wanted to back out but he said it was too late and now I had to tell him what it was. I felt like back peddling but I couldn't, he knew I had something on my mind and would not give up until I shared it.

I waited anxiously and prayerfully until his arrival. He came and I showed him to the couch where I shared how much I cared for him and enjoyed being with him and what he meant to me. I was shaking a bit and he tried to comfort me. Whatever it is I could tell him, he said. I told him it might cause him to break up with me and that scared me but he didn't feel as though anything I could say would make him do that. So, what I did was give him a seven and a half page letter I had written years earlier with my testimony and let him read it. I told him I would be upstairs until he finished. I went to my room and lay across my bed, praying and waiting. I listened for the front door to open and close or footsteps coming up the stairs. Time went by and I grew more nervous, I heard nothing.

After what seemed to be an eternity, I slowly eased down the stairs, peeking for him, trying to get some sense of how he was taking the news. I got nothing. I was so ashamed. I didn't know what to do. Momma never prepared me for days like this and as I tell my students, you never want to put yourself in a situation where you risk losing someone you love or really care about because of something that could have been prevented.

When I reached him, he looked up at me and I quickly looked away at the floor. He told me to come and sit down next to him. I did, but I couldn't look at him. He gave me a comforting hug. Now what was said after that is a little fuzzy to me, but I'll do my best.

He was very calm. I think it was probably from shock. He was being a man and holding it all together. He just held me and ran his fingers through my hair. I showed him the paperwork from my test so that he could read it for himself.

He asked me what it all meant because he didn't know exactly what he was looking at, having never seen anything like it before. I did my best to explain what it meant and how it lined up with God's promise of healing through the blood of his son Jesus (Isaiah 53:5).

He made it clear that he didn't want to break up with me. That was great news. That day I felt loved and accepted. It's what I had been waiting for forever.

We dated for several months after that and he didn't treat me any differently than before. He was not afraid to touch me or kiss me. After a while, however, he wanted more. He wanted a more recent negative test result. I didn't fault him for that, it's only right. I felt the pressure to get this for him so I scheduled a doctor's appointment. Before I had the chance to get to the doctor, the guy and I had broken up.

I believed in my healing, but I needed to know how strong his faith in God was. This is not a fun place to be worrying about how someone is going to react. Will they harm you, will they care, or will they leave you? You just don't know.

God had separated us because I had made man my God and gotten off track.

Even as I teach abstinence today, I tell students that it's their right to know their partner's status and to get tested. I tell the students that if the person they are dating has a problem with getting tested that should send up a red flag that perhaps that person is trying to hide something. In this day and age it should be the norm that you will be asked to take a test and/or show proof of a recent test. It does not say that one doesn't trust the person or want to be with them, it is simply to put both minds at ease.

A person can be infected with a sexually transmitted disease and not know it and pass it along to you. Many of the sexually transmitted diseases don't show symptoms. That is very scary because you can have a disease for years and not know unless you are being tested.

We tell students that if they are having sex they should get tested regularly. However, if they want to avoid having to worry about contracting a sexually transmitted disease, they can practice abstinence.

Abstinence is saving yourself for marriage. It means you choose to not take part in any sexual activity until marriage; you marry an uninfected partner by getting tested and then remain faithful in that relationship. This approach is frowned upon and dismissed by many in society; however, we are working to change the perception. Abstinence is an option even if you've previously been sexually active.

What society has to recognize is that sex is more than just a physical thing. It involves the mind, the emotions and social aspects of a person. Sex impacts the whole person.

I've heard people say they know someone who has had sex for years with their mate and have never gotten pregnant or a sexually transmitted disease. I tell them that even if a person did get an STD and are experiencing symptoms such as burning, itching or pain upon urination, they are not likely to tell you.

Then there is the emotional side to being sexually active that we must take into account. Even if a person doesn't get pregnant or contract a sexually transmitted infection, they will become emotionally attached to the person they are having sex with. This happens due to a hormone called oxytocin which is released during sexual activity and acts as a bonding agent between the partners. So if the relationship ends, you may still be tied to this person for days, months, even years to come. You can still experience hurt or pain upon seeing the person or even the mention of their name. We tell our students that this is often worse than the physical consequences because it plays on a person's self-esteem and self-worth. It can lead to a life pattern of always being taken advantage of and other unhealthy types of relationships.

I tell young people my story of how I got caught up having sex as a teen, but at age eighteen, I made the decision to practice abstinence. I tell them it is not easy and that it takes commitment and work to set physical boundaries in their relationships. They must communicate those boundaries to the people they date and remember not to put themselves in compromising situations. I let them know that I have stood by my commitment and will keep it until I marry.

I speak of how I wished someone would have told me about abstinence and the dangers of sex when I was their age because I could have been saved from a lot of pain. I count it a privilege and an honor to share this lifesaving message with young people and adults who will listen.

Too many times we have learned of people going into relationships and marriages blind.

They didn't get tested initially and when they are tested, they test positive for STDS including HIV. It is not fair and we must change this.

There are no set criteria for how or when to divulge your status, but if you are going to engage in sexual activity you are obligated to tell and if you don't, you can be legally prosecuted if found out. Other than that you must decide when it is the right time. I personally think it should be before you get too emotionally involved.

Within the first month or so of my relationship, I wanted to tell. I felt uneasy, however, so I gave it some time to test out his character and find out where he was coming from. I wanted to know if I could trust him with such personal information. However, as soon as I saw the relationship going somewhere, I had to tell it. I think it is the best thing to do even though you run the risk of being rejected. That person has the right to know what they are getting into and to decide if they want to pursue a relationship. I regret having put myself in that position in the first place, but unfortunately, it does happen when we make poor choices.

In classes, questions have come up and I

answer to the best of my ability without divulging my deepest secrets. I struggled with that as well but because of the laws that prevent me from being able to openly discuss my religious beliefs in the secular class settings, I refrain from going too deep into my personal story. I really can't do my story justice without mentioning my Lord and how God has brought me through.

Over the years, I have received many words of exhortation, encouragement and prophesy. A word spoken at the right time can mean the difference between life and death, quitting or running on. The words spoken in my life kept me going, believing and hoping. God has also spoken to me personally during prayer, dreams and visions and during meditation.

€

Letter to God

God, I remember when the pain was so great I couldn't bear it, I felt as though no one knew or could comprehend feeling as if your heart was beaten, twisted, about to fall out of your chest, but you were there. I felt like I was dying. I could hardly breathe. At times I was gasping for air. I ached and hurt so bad. I could hardly move at times and I felt like I should be lying in a hospital bed hooked up to a bunch of medical equipment. I knew within my spirit God was with me and this was an attack of the enemy. I was deceived momentarily into thinking that this was it for me.

God help me to accept all that I am and shall be for your glory. Help me not to reject the gifts or calling you have placed within me. Thank you Lord Jesus. I give you all the glory, the entire honor and the praise in your name. I love you Lord so much. Thank you for who you are and for making me, who I am! Love you Daddy.

See, I felt like no one cared, but you did. I felt all alone, but you were there. My body ached with unspeakable, indescribable pain, but yet and still I had to go on like nothing was wrong. I still prayed, I still attended church and actively participated. I still worked and assisted in the home and for those who ask how I could? Jesus is all I can really say.

I held on to hope that one day it would all end and the pain would go away. Many nights I cried myself to sleep and whenever I could during the day, you would hear me praying, crying and talking to you. In the midst of it all, I mus-

tered up a sacrificial praise.

When you are physically hurting it does something to you emotionally and if it's not stopped, it can contaminate your spirit. God, you rocked me in your arms, wiped my tears and soothed me to sleep. You allowed this trial and even though you alone are able to call it to naught at any given moment, you have not yet for some reason. I have gained much strength, patience, faith, longsuffering, meekness, humbleness, knowledge, wisdom, understanding and love, which are great tools to run this Christian race.

I welcomed any sign of normalcy. My monthly reminder, the visitor we women love to hate and sometimes pray to see coming, was welcomed. For a while it was all I had to look forward to because it let me know I was still human and alive. There were times I felt less than human, like dirt, but lower, so unworthy. This is not the way God wanted or designed me to feel. In Psalm 139, he tells me that I am fearfully and wonderfully made. In Genesis, it states that everything God created was good.

So when the enemy put condemning, negative thoughts in your mind, you can immediately dismiss them because you know that it will never be from God. He does not talk like that or think like that at all. Remember our thoughts are not His thoughts nor our ways, His ways.

CHAPTER FIVE

How I Came To Be

Now that you have learned so much about my battles and triumphs, I want to give you some background on who I am and what made me the person that I have become.

I was born and raised in South Florida. I grew up in what is all too common, a single-parent home. My mom played a dual role as mother and father for my two brothers and myself. I am the middle child. My younger brother and I are thirteen years apart. I believe my mom did a great job raising us on her own. She instilled within me strength, faith and perseverance.

As a young child, I attended public elementary and middle school. My high school became a magnet school my freshman year. My high school career was a crazy time for me because I was a shy girl that never really felt like I fitted in anywhere. I had friends and there were boys who liked me but I didn't know how to respond, so I never had a real, steady relationship.

When I was fifteen and about to begin my sophomore year of high school, I experienced a very traumatic event, I was raped by a twenty-two year-old man. I endured going through a criminal trial where he was sentenced to a year and a day in jail. He was allowed to plead guilty to a lesser charge of lewd and lascivious acts on a minor. Like in so many rape cases, the defense attorney tried to put me on trial. The man who raped me claimed that he could produce other guys with whom I had been sexually active, which was not true. The medical evidence proved the facts and God knew the truth, which in the end is all that matters. Undoubtedly, this experience would affect me for the rest of my life. During my sophomore year, I took ill and spent nearly three months out of school. I ended up on homebound education.

After returning to school for my junior and senior years, I made the honor roll and managed to have a core group of friends who took their education seriously as well. Still, I felt weird and out of place. I was extremely shy and because my mom did not have much money I was unable to participate in many of the school activities.

I began working at age fourteen and have worked ever since. I used my money to help support the home. What my mom wasn't able to provide materially she made up for with love and care. I was spoiled with home cooked breakfast in the mornings and dinner each evening.

I had the great privilege of attending Florida State University after graduating from high school. I had a tough time leaving home. When I went off to college, I remember while my mother and brothers were trying to get me settled into my dorm room, I changed my mind and told them I was going back home with them. When they finally left, I locked myself in my room and cried. I felt like I had made this terrible mistake and I wanted to run after them. This lasted for about two days and then a knock on the door and an invitation to hang out brought me out of my funk.

I spent my first semester getting acclimated to this newfound freedom. I ended up on academic probation because I had terrible study skills and could not successfully balance all of the freedom I had gained. My second semester,

I took ill and decided to sit the semester out. I went back home to the astonishment of all my family and friends because they knew me to be a serious student who loved school. I went back to college in the fall and finished my under-graduate degree in four and a half years. I earned a Bachelor of Science degree in Elemen-tary Education with honors.

After graduation, I came home for the sum-mer. I had every intention of returning to Talla-hassee where I graduated college. I was offered a job as an elementary school teacher by the school where I interned. However, my mom be-came very ill and had to have triple bypass sur-gery. I stayed to take care of her and my younger brother.

Time went on and I got stuck. I attempted to leave several times but just could not bring my-self to do it. So, I took a teaching position as an interim teacher for an elementary school. This proved to be too difficult because I had also started the graduate program at a local univer-sity. I was in an inner-city school and with the demands of home, school and work it took its toll and I became ill. I decided to give up teach-ing full time and just work as a substitute teacher.

While enrolled in the graduate program, I also accepted a job as a secretary with the university. Ultimately, I decided to quit my full time job as well as graduate school so that I could care for my mom and younger brother.

Over the last few years, I have come to know myself and understand why I grew up this shy, withdrawn, scared little girl. I was very afraid of people and the world around me. This came to be from past sexual abuse as an infant, child and teen. I was molested by a relative as an infant and it affected the way in which I viewed the world and people. I know this happened because of the way I have always been uncomfortable around him, never wanting to be near him or be touched by him. I also had a vivid dream some years ago of a man standing over my crib and having violated me. I asked God what it meant but it would be a couple of years before I got an understanding. God allows us to grasp things when we are ready to handle them and He was just preparing me with that dream.

As a teen, I was molested by a family friend who was later prosecuted for doing this to many other young people. The only thing I did in this case was give my story to an investigator. They had plenty of evidence of their own so I did not need to take part in a trial, thank God. I know that other things such as an absentee father played a role in shaping me as well. It's a great feeling just knowing why I am who I am. I am free to move on from here.

I have grown in leaps and bounds in the past several years so anyone meeting me now couldn't possibly comprehend how far I've come. I am so grateful to God for loving me so much as to give me a new lease on life. He set me free from my past and from myself. I feel as though I've just started living even though I accepted Christ as my Lord and Savior in December of 1993. I still allowed myself to be held in bondage because of my lack of knowledge.

At this point in my life I am learning more about me everyday and how good God is. How intelligent and all-powerful He is. I am appreciating each and every trial He has allowed me to go through to make and mold me into His image.

CHAPTER SIX

Trusting the Lord

Lord Jesus I thank you for my overcoming every obstacle. I thank you that no weapon formed against me shall prosper. God I thank you for discernment, thank you for victory, I thank you for teaching, and showing me that every time I get a word of confirmation or prophesy the enemy's job is to come in, steal it and discourage me. He wants to make me doubt and he is very vigilant at this. I get feelings of being overwhelmed, like I can't accomplish what you said I could and I thank the Holy Ghost for teaching me that it is not God speaking these things to me but the devil.

If God spoke it, He is well able to do it, to bring it to pass in my life and He didn't base his decision to speak the words of hope, purpose and promise into my life based on my ability or strength but on His. If only I would let go and let God, surrender all to him, lay everything aside and say, "Here I am Lord use me and send me. Have your way in me and through me.

Use my body as a vessel to bring about your plan and purpose in the land. O, I release myself Jesus. Lord God, I crucify this old stinky flesh in Jesus Name."

In December 2003 and actually throughout the entire holiday season, I was terribly ill. I was embarrassed by my looks even though people said nothing to my face. I had lost a lot of weight and was in severe pain, tormented emotionally and mentally. My spirit was vexed within me. I had recently endured a break up with the only man I'd ever shared so much of me with. I had even shared my deepest secrets with him. He had filled my head with dreams of marriage and family. I felt literally like my world was coming to an end, like I was dying from heartbreak and illness that seemed to plague my body. Day in and day out, I hurt inside and out. It was a chore to shower and get dressed. When I listened to the radio, I cried. Everything made me cry. I could hardly eat. I allowed the enemy to torment me. Because I had been in an unhealthy relationship, I felt as though I was being punished. I learned this was not the case.

One day at work, I was full of despair and a

co-worker agreed to pray with me. We went to an empty office, shut the door and she prayed. God began to speak through her telling her that He understood what I was going through and how confused I was. God knew that I wanted answers and I wanted to understand, but He said that I needed to trust Him. He said that what I was going through was not punishment for something I had done in my past but it had to happen. It was suppose to be this way and a scripture (Matthew 9:17), came up "How can you put new wine into old wine skins?"

I was very touched by this prayer and God's message to me. I left the room encouraged and grateful for my family of God.

For the Christmas season, I had money to shop but it meant very little because I was ill, and in pain. Like my Pastor has said many times, you can have all the money in the world but if you don't have good health, it means nothing. Your health is your wealth. You must have good health and strength to enjoy the money.

I can remember going into Wal-Mart to Christmas shop barely able to walk. It was such a chore to push the cart up and down the aisles. We take so much for granted because here I was struggling to do such routine tasks. I was a mess but God on the inside of me helped me to continue to praise Him in spite of how I felt or looked. Through it all, I trusted Him. He was all I had and all I needed. I cried and prayed and hoped for relief. It appeared that it would never come.

When I pulled into my driveway, I looked at the steps it took for me to get to the front door and reach to unlock it and I felt defeated; however, I knew I had to do it in order to get to bed. So with God's help, I did it.

At night, I turned my face to the wall and prayed like my brother Hezekiah (2 Kings 20:2-3). I reminded God of His word and promises concerning me. A few times, I was short of breath and I was fearful. I had the devil whispering in my ear, speaking death to me and I had to combat those thoughts with God's word.

I could not do this on my own, my strength was weak. The bible tells us that when we are weak, God is made strong within us, (2 Cor. 12:10) and that we can do all things through Christ who strengthens us (Philippians 4:13).

One of my all time favorite verses, Jeremiah

29:11 states, "For I know the thoughts I think toward you saith the Lord, thoughts of peace and not of evil, to give you an expected end." This scripture kept me encouraged, and taught me that any negativity coming at me was not of God because He only has good thoughts concerning me and my life.

Abraham, a true inspiration and role model for me, has been a tremendous blessing. He was a friend of God who hoped against hope. He had a promise from God that seemed impossible to man. It took many years to come to fruition, but yet he held on and it did come to past. I love the stories of Abraham and his great faith. God gave us His word to encourage us, to teach us and to keep us until we reach home.

With all that I experienced during the month of December, it now seems appropriate that in December 2003 I received a word from a favorite minister of mine about me singing, doing praise and worship. I love singing and praising the Lord, but I've never considered myself to be a good singer. I just really got into the praise doing church services, and I always sung at home, in the car and at work. My praise has kept me!

I was told that I would lead the people in praise and worship to the Lord. I was instructed to get some music tracks together, practice and get going. At first, I kind of laughed at the thought of my shy little self singing and leading praise and worship. Within myself I was thinking this minister has been right before with words from the Lord for me, however, maybe this time she missed it. I mean come on, me, sing?

A week or so went by and it kept coming back to my remembrance. I wanted to be obedient to God; I can't afford not to be. But being obedient to God also means being obedient to His servants.

Reluctantly, I went out and got a couple of tracks from the local Christian bookstore. Days later I told my Pastor that I was working on a couple of songs. This was during the Christmas season and I was going through a rough patch with bouts of excruciating pain, loss of breath, and the enemy speaking defeat and death.

We were in a revival during the Christmas season and I went to the services with my body racked in pain because I didn't know what else to do. God was the only one who could give me relief. The woman of God, not knowing my situation at all, spoke to me. She instructed me to stay close to the anointing. She also said that the spiritual growth that I was experiencing was just the beginning of what God was going to do in my life.

"He is going to do something awesome in your life, the thing He promised you. That *thing* is being manifested. He's going to do it for you. It's a done deal, His loves penetrates all throughout your fiber tonight."

Physically, I felt better after that meeting. God had begun a work of restoration. Almost immediately after that meeting we were in another meeting with an awesome, anointed woman of God. She did not know me from Adam, as the old folk say. She knew nothing of me but God used her to speak into my life. Under the anointing of God she spoke.

"God wants to deliver you from sickness and disease. We are binding it in the name of Jesus, and whatever is bound on earth is bound in heaven; we bind the spirit of darkness. God is setting you free; He is breaking mindsets. He says you've been bound too long, way too long. Whom the Son sets free is free indeed. God says your diagnosis is a lie. We bind sickness and disease and infirmity and we loose health and life. He is delivering you from your past. We call you whole in the name of Jesus and your body to line up with the word of God, health spring forth. What is broken is being mended and what has been torn is being corrected. As Jesus spoke to Lazareth to come forth and shake off those grave clothes (John 11:43-44), He is speaking to you."

Why am I sharing this? I want you to understand that if you stay in God, He will give you exactly what you need to make it through whatever situation you find yourself in. I was able to go home and rest, actually have a good night sleep after that night. I had been unable to rest for days on end because I was vexed in my spirit and in my body, but God touched me that night and delivered me.

It's not that you need someone else to speak to you all the time because God will speak directly to you if you will listen. It's just that sometimes you can get so full and burdened down with the cares of life that it's noisy. You can't hear from Him and you need to hear a word to encourage you to run on, to remind you of His promises and to let you know you're going to make it.

Many of the words spoken over my life blessed me because they were future tense. Meaning they referred to my future and that was enough for me. It signified to me that what God had already spoken was coming and that I wasn't going anywhere until every word was fulfilled. It helped me to realize that despite the pain and the heartache of the moment, there was a brighter day coming. He meant it for my good. If I could just hold on, this too shall pass. I have lived my life like this, looking ahead for a brighter day and that brighter day is coming.

As the year was coming to an end, my pastor asked me to sing at our New Year's Eve service. The enemy was speaking to me telling me that I couldn't sing, that I wouldn't be able to keep up with the demands of being a worship leader. He questioned where I was going to get materials from? I fought through with prayer and reading the Word. Whenever I was in the Word, I got relief from pain and I received strength and encouragement.

The day I was to sing, I was not well. The enemy spoke, saying that as soon as I took the microphone and attempted to sing, I was going to drop dead in the pulpit. He even showed me a picture in my mind's eye. I did become a bit fearful. But with God's help, I decided I would rather obey His word and die while doing what I had been moved to do. So I took the microphone and sang and I survived the experience. This was in 2003 and I am still singing today. It has meant so much to me and it's been such a blessing.

The bible tells us that God dwells in the praises of His people. I know that leading praise and worship has kept me and been a huge part of my survival. At times when I didn't feel like praising God because of physical and emotional sickness, I had to praise Him because I have been charged to do so. The enemy can't stand for people to praise God, so he does not stay when there is true praise and worship going on.

I have had the experience of visiting the doctor and receiving negative reports, yet I have gone to church to lead praise and worship. I can remember crying one particular time when I was so disappointed that my report was not what I expected. I was expecting to be released from medications, but that wasn't the case, so I went to church all downtrodden and yet I had to sing. I walked out and took the microphone, closed my eyes and tears began flowing. I opened my mouth to sing and tried to make the tears stop falling, but I couldn't. It was obvious something was bothering me because I was crying and the song hadn't even started so I couldn't play it off. I told no one what was up. I just spoke to the Lord, my friend. I apologized to Him for my weak moment even though I knew He understood me and what I was feeling. On the second song, I cut loose with praise worthy of my Lord who is able to do the impossible. Delay doesn't mean denial. He is still God and shall do what He said He would do, if I hold on and trust Him. All Glory to Him!

CHAPTER SEVEN

Standing On God's Promise

In the spring of 2004, we had a Women's Conference at my church one weekend. I had been out of it spiritually, physically, emotionally and mentally. However, I attended the conference not sure what I would get out of it, but I was hopeful. I had an awesome time. We had guests fly in from several states and local musical guests as well.

During one of the services, the praise and worship was high and I got caught up. The Lord began to deal with me and show me things that were to come in my future, like marriage and ministry. At some point I got lost in the praise and a loud, blood curdling cry came up from my belly, my soul and it shook people including myself. However, I couldn't stop it. Something was breaking loose. I can remember my pastor saying that it was okay and that it had to happen, in fact it needed to happen. In the midst of my screaming and praising, I fell out on the floor, crying and weeping and praising the Lord.

A visiting Evangelist spoke to me saying I would never be the same after that day. It was so true. Something broke in the spirit realm for me that day that I can't explain but from that day to this one, I changed.

Now I know many people reading this will say it does not take all that to praise God, that it is unnecessary. I respect your opinion; however, it takes that for me. I have questioned God in times past about the manner in which I praise Him and my church praises Him. I am comfortable in an environment where people may strike out running around the church at any moment, speak in tongues (heavenly language), and fall out under the spirit, the laying of hands, prophecy, and ministering. It is where I fit.

I asked God why I ended up in this kind of ministry and whether it is wrong. I received the answer that it is not wrong. You are doing what is in you to do, was my answer. You were placed here and it's where you belong. I cannot see myself any other way but praising and worshipping God with the freedom to let go and let God. I don't play church because I fear and reverence God too much for that. I will not do something unless I am moved by the Lord to do so and that is how it should be with all people. What feels right for the individual and is in line with His word, which should be the basis of our actions.

We have examples in the bible of people who are radical in their praise of God. David danced out of his clothes before the Lord (2 Samuel 6:14). I think the bottom line is you are placed where you are supposed to be and what fits for one person may not fit for another. You must always be true to yourself and God. One way does not mean better than another. We must worship in spirit and in truth, which is what God seeks.

This topic reminds me of a beautiful older woman I met who was Seventh Day Adventist. We had such great times of fellowship together. I loved talking with her and learning from her. We did not waste time speaking on our differences, but what we shared in common, which was our love for Christ, our faith in His power to do the impossible.

She shared with me how people worship God in different ways. She said that some may cry quietly in there seats or lift a hand in the air.

Some may clap their hands, dance or sing. It is all okay, one way is no better than another. It's just that God created us differently and so we will not all worship in the same way and it does not mean that the person who runs and shouts their praises is feeling the Lord anymore than the person sitting and crying quietly. That was wisdom that I valued from this woman of God. I will never forget it.

In August of 2004, I came forward with my testimony before my church and the report which indicated that the HIV was not found in my body. My mom witnessed the report a few months before her passing.

I was compelled by God to tell it. I spoke to my church family about how the enemy had me in bondage for years because of my lack of knowledge. I spoke about how I knew what God's word said about healing; however I did not walk in it. I had what a favorite minister of mine refers to as "head faith" and not "heart faith." In other words, I had been taught that by His stripes I was healed and I believed that word when it was preached, however, I had not allowed that word to take root in my heart so that it could work for me.

There was a period of a couple of weeks where I prepared myself to tell my story. It was a bit nerve wracking. I spent some sleepless nights praying and meditating. I wondered how it would be received. I didn't tell friends or family I was going to do this because I did not want to be talked out of it. I felt it was something I needed to do.

Many times before I had talked myself out of sharing for fear of bringing shame to my family, but I had to realize this was not about me or them. It is about my Savior. He deserves the glory and the honor for all He has done in my life. If I keep silent I help no one. Others need to know how good God is. We all need to know that God is faithful and trustworthy. We all need to know that God is our best friend to the end and that it is His will to heal.

I acquired several tiny paperback booklets on healing written by T. L. Osborne and Marilyn Hickey from the Christian bookstore that were very timely. The books taught me that it was God's will to heal and it was my right to receive the healing. I was taught how to keep my healing and not let the enemy steal it back by using the examples given in those books.

Many people, including me, believed that sometimes it is God's will for us to suffer sickness. Many times people refer to the scripture about Paul having a thorn in his side and they say it was sickness. However, if you search it out, that thorn was a messenger of Satan sent to torment him, to discourage him from continuing on in the faith. All the scriptures point to God healing folks. Before you go there, let me say I have read in the New Testament how some people did not receive healing, but that was due to their unbelief, not Jesus' inability to heal. He is able!

If He bore our sicknesses on the cross, why would He then turn around and give them back to us? (Isaiah 53:4-5) He traveled throughout the different countries healing those that were sick.

Now the Word does not tell us we won't ever get sick, however, we choose whether or not we remain sick. Where is your faith? Do you really believe God to be a healer? We have to take some responsibility as well for the way we take care of our bodies. Are we eating right? Do we exercise? Are we watching what we allow into our bodies? Then there is also that *old sin thing* in this world that we have to watch as well. I can say that I *know* God is a healer.

After telling my testimony, I was applauded for my bravery. It was all a GOD thing! There is no way I could have gotten up and said a thing without knowing He was with me and on my side. My pastor just blessed me by loving on me and supporting me always through her prayers and words of wisdom.

That day I gained freedom from the stronghold the enemy had over me by the mere fact that I was keeping such a huge secret. It was as if a large, grey cloud lifted from over my head. I came into the Light. The devil could no longer oppress me because I no longer wondered who knew and who didn't know. Also, what I thought was going to be so bad, was not. I received love. I was not treated differently or unfairly. I felt accepted, which is what every human desires.

I must pause here for a moment and say however, that it was a little weird that no one said anything to me about it. It was as if, to them, it never happened. There have been times when I wished people would say something, acknowledge my struggle, and give me a listening ear or shoulder to cry on. I realized after a while that most people just don't know what to say or how to handle it.

I told a couple of people that it would help to have an example of someone who had come through victoriously. It would help to hear how they did it but unfortunately due to how certain diseases are stereotyped, this was not within reach for me. This is one of the main reasons I write my story as well. I want to help someone who's out there as I was. I was searching for help. I was looking for examples of people who had overcome the disease and I desperately needed the inspiration that their triumph would provide for me.

We need to see people being healed of this virus. It's not that we walk by sight; we are to walk by faith. However, having a personal example of healing, as well as the examples of healing in the bible, does helps. It is difficult but not impossible to walk out on nothing, to launch out into the deep in unchartered waters. I've spent many days praying about this very thing, asking for examples.

I have been lied on, criticized and hurt. I've

had family members to discuss my life amongst themselves and judge me, which of course bothered me. Thanks to God; I got over it quickly with His help. I forgive them because they just misunderstood me and what God was doing with my life. I did not understand where God was taking me or what He was doing. God has just kept me hidden in His arms under His feathers.

I know that I have been overlooked by men because of my diagnosis. You get the blank stares and whispers and I would be lying if I said it didn't faze me a time or two. There have been guys interested in me and then started asking around about why I'm still single and then they changed their mind.

Church members, family and friends have turned people away from talking to me and it hurt sometimes, but again, I can't blame them. They have to do what they think is best. I just wished they would trust me to do the right thing and tell it for myself. I would never put anyone in a situation to hurt them and I just wished people would know that about me.

God has a plan and when the time is right, He will send my Boaz. Until then, I must wait and prepare myself. I have to get moving and work with the ministry God has for me.

God continues to use His people to make a difference in my life. I remember when out of the blue I received an invitation to go to a concert featuring the gospel singer Donald Lawrence. He is one of my favorite artists because his songs speak life, and they are full of the word of God and His promises. I get strength and encouragement from his music as well as other artists. I jumped at the opportunity not realizing that I had a divine appointment to be there. My life changed for the better that night unbeknownst to me.

I had a ball praising the Lord. I heard songs I hadn't heard before like *"Giants," "Encourage Yourself"* and *"The Blessings of Abraham."* I don't know where I could've been to have missed those great songs, but I was blessed to hear them.

God spoke to me that night through those songs. He showed me how I was to inherit the blessings of Abraham, how to go and get it, even through the man of God speaking over our lives. I had to break out into praise even though he or the people may not have known why I had to shout and yell out praises, God knew.

He showed me some things in the spirit like my book being written, my ministry, my home, finances, and children. I got a glimpse and heard him speak to my spirit that I was going to get the promises He made to me. I was so blessed and on a spiritual high that I went out the next day and sacrificially bought his new CD. I boomed it in my car all weekend.

Now here is the real kicker. When I got to the third track on his CD, I heard a testimony and could hardly believe how awesome God is. How He is so providential and so smart to have me in the right place at the right time to get what I needed to get.

The testimony I speak of was of a young man who had tested positive for HIV a year before me and went through the many medications and the related frustrations. He went in to the doctor years later and received a negative test result. Hallelujah! In order to clear the doubts of any naysayer, the doctors conducted a battery of tests that clearly indicated the virus was not in his system at all.

I danced and shouted in my car so loud. I cried and hollered and sung praises to my God.

He is not a respecter of person and what he does for one he'll do for two and that means you. I called up a friend and played it for her. I was so excited. Now I had a reference to what I've been living and hoping for. And wouldn't you know it, not long after this, I saw the brother on TBN, a Christian television network, where he offered more of his testimony.

The testimony on the CD does not do his story justice even though it is such a blessing. Because of the limited space available for the music, I understand that he couldn't tell it all. However, it was awesome to hear him share openly and honestly about what he had gone through. It's something special that takes place when you hear about someone that has gone through what you are dealing with and come out successfully. There is deliverance that takes place.

He spoke about opportunistic infections, symptoms, multiple positive test results and hearing this made his story more real to me. I thank God for this brother. He said something that day that motivated me even more to write this book. He said that the world needs to hear these stories of triumph over this disease. People need to step forward and say, "Hey, I've been through what you're going through and I'm here to tell you, you can come out, you can overcome, and you can receive healing."

Over the years there were many times I would go to church feeling faint, full of pain and tormented mentally, but I never gave up because God never gave up on me. There were many times I wondered if anyone saw what I was going through. I felt embarrassed by my looks. I now realize a lot of this was in my mind. At times, I could hardly breathe, I felt like I was slipping away. I would reach out to grab a pew just to maintain my balance. I would take deep breaths to make sure I was still breathing. It was only God that was sustaining me. He gave me the strength and desire to keep going. I always felt like one day I would share my experiences with others to the Glory of God.

So again, you can understand why I was so moved by the brother who tested negative and urged others to tell their stories of triumph. I too want to let people know God is real! He is a keeper if you want to be kept. He is a best friend, the best you could ever have. You can't go wrong with God in your life and on your side.

As I write this section today, there is a light shining on the paper as I sit at my desk. God is here and well pleased. He wants you to know He loves you and He cares. He cares about everything concerning you. He understands you better than you understand yourself (Psa.139). He just wants you to trust Him, trust Him with your life. He knows what's best for you. Glory to God! Hallelujah!

The song *Hallelujah* is ringing in my spirit. The time is here for God's children to rise up and take a stand for righteousness, for holiness. It is time for you to live for Christ, to do what he asks you to do, to fulfill your pre-ordained destiny. You must fulfill the purpose for which you were put on this earth. Glory to God! Have your way Jesus! "For the hour cometh and now is where the true worshippers must worship Him in spirit and in truth." (John 4:23)

Reflections

Jesus, I often think of how awesome it is that I am still alive. Many have gone on, but God kept me alive. I have to know it is for a reason. In Psalm 118:17, it states "I shall not die, but live, and declare the works of the Lord." I have stood on this word many a day. In my asking God why I'm still alive and how is it that this little, well not so little now, body of mine could go through so much and still keep functioning? How is it that no matter what report I get or pain I feel, no matter the disappointments, no matter the wait, how am I able to keep going? The answer is that Jesus, deep, deep, deep down on the inside won't allow me to quit.

Many times I felt like throwing my hands up, but God wouldn't let me. He kept me in remembrance of His promises to me. I pray that you will allow God to get so deep within the crevices of your soul that come what may you will stand as the word instructs us to do in Ephesians 6:13.

It amazes me how far God has brought me. I am so blessed and grateful to Him. He has given me a second chance, and in some things; I've been given more than a second chance to get it right. I want to thank you Jesus for the many chances that you have granted me. He is so faithful and loving, He is longsuffering and I see more and more each day how smart He is.

I have been very hard on myself. I've beaten myself up with words and thoughts, saying I should've done this or that, or I should be farther along but I realize that God knows what He is doing. He knows exactly what it is going to take to get me where I need to be.

I now know why we are to lean not unto our own understanding but acknowledge Him in all our ways so that He may direct our paths. I feel like I should be doing more at times and then I feel like I'm doing too much. I have to pray and talk to God about it.

€

I'm writing this book for several reasons. I am not my own, I've been bought with a price, the blood of my Jesus and I write this book to Glorify Him, my Lord and Savior. I want to help somebody find Him, and develop a relationship with Him. I want people to come to know Him as real because no matter your situation, He can help. Jesus can turn it around for your good. I want to let others that may be going through what I have gone through or something similar, know that they are not alone. I felt so alone many times and had to rely on Jesus to comfort me, to listen to me and be my friend.

I used to be so consumed with times and places and doctor appointments and people. I am free! I'm no longer consumed with those things everyday. I am no longer walking around in an oppressed state of existence. I'm not overwhelmed with questions of what if? Who if? When it comes to my health, I just am. I'm just striving to fulfill my purpose in Christ and to receive the manifestation of all He has promised me.

I asked God the question. "How do you get the promises to manifest from the spirit realm to the natural where we can touch them?"

The answer I received is that we must become so consumed with God and we must be busy about doing God's work instead of allowing our situation to consume us, causing us to feel oppressed and defeated.

God has to become our reality more so than what we see before us. God is more real than any situation we may face and we must acknowledge that and live in Him. For the bible declares that it is in God that we live, move and have our being (Acts 17:28). When we do this, our problems will fade away amidst His glory in our lives.

I want to encourage you and let you know I feel your pain, your anguish and frustration and I pray you will allow God to take it away and strengthen you.

I am special because He made me in His image and likeness. However, you are special too. My bible tells me God is no respecter of person. In other words, what He did for me, He will do for you (Acts 10:34). You can count on it, you just have to believe.

What I have written may seem farfetched to some, and I questioned it as I wrote the words. Will they believe what I am writing? However, I must tell you that it is the truth.

I have spent too many years wishing it all away but I'm done with that. I can't change my past, what's done is done. As my mom always said to me as I was growing up, "What's done in the dark, will come to light."

Here it is! I must move forward and embrace what God has given me, *new life!* I must learn from my past, share the blessings with others and go on in Christ to fulfill my destiny in Him.

What I want you, the reader, to see while reading this is that Jesus is at the center of it all. I pray that my story will point you to God.

There is so much to tell that I just can't tell it all. But please know that it is because God lives that I live and because He is, I am and the same can be true for you.

It is vital that you get connected to a Word church, a church where the whole word of God is preached and practiced, where your faith can be built up. The bible teaches that faith cometh by hearing and hearing by the word of God. God can make what is impossible with man, possible (Matthew 19:26).

I'm going to trust in God

I spent too much of my time hiding medicines and then sneaking to take them, always looking over my shoulder. Lots of time and energy has been wasted worrying about what others thought, how they would react and what they would say. It was not easy keeping this from roommates or co-workers when I had to take off from work early or come in late because of doctor appointments, picking up medications from the clinic, or getting lab work done.

I wore two faces because I would go into work or school as if everything was normal even though I had just gone through things some people would rather die than go through. I was able to manage and remain pleasant only by the grace of God.

I know it is only due to God's strength because I would have thrown in the towel a long time ago. I thought about it a few times but only for a moment because greater is He that is in me than he that is in the world. I had to come to the realization that what I was going through was so much bigger than me. It wasn't about me. I was just a vessel God chose to use to show forth His glory as He has done time and time again with countless other individuals.

I'll never forget some of my experiences. I can remember wrapping pills in aluminum foil or tissue to hide them. I spent countless hours ripping labels off medicine bottles and tearing them into little bits and dispersing them sometimes in separate bags, in separate places to keep people from putting the pieces together. I recognize now that the enemy had me in bondage. I lived in constant fear which is not the will of God.

I would find clever ways to sneak drinks to take my medicine. When I had a roommate in the same room with me, it was difficult. Also, it could be frustrating to schedule times to take medication around my school and work schedule. I hated having to make myself stay awake just to take a few pills.

I remember coming home from a long hard day of work and school, preparing dinner, putting my brother to bed and wanting to just crash, but I couldn't because it's not time to take my medicine yet. I have to wait a couple hours. If you've been in this position, I feel you. Nevertheless, God is good!

One thing I want people to understand is that when people look mean or upset or crazy you shouldn't judge them because you don't know what they are dealing with at the time. I know many times people have thought I was weird, mean or finicky not knowing that I was in pain either physically, emotionally, spiritually or all of them. I can think of a great example.

I remember being in a wedding for a friend of mine. During this time I was going through a bout of sickness, pain and torment. Walking down the aisle was hard for me. I felt faint and had sharp pains. The enemy was speaking death in my ear. Even though I thought I was covering up well someone later told me I looked very sad. They thought it was because I wanted to be married. If only that was the reason. I was sorry I portrayed that image.

Another reason people may look unapproachable is abuse. Survivors of sexual abuse can behave standoffish for fear of being hurt again, of being abandoned or rejected or misunderstood.

I am in the process of healing from my past which involved emotional, verbal and sexual abuse. I'm discovering and understanding why all my life I've felt out of place, rejected and ashamed for everything. It's a very emotional process, but very necessary. God is with me and He knew the time would come when I would be ready to go through this process and I truly thank Him for his infinite wisdom and divine providence.

His word is true that his ways are not our ways and his thoughts are not our thoughts. I would have never chosen to go this route on my own. I was of the perspective that God is my counselor and indeed He is. However God puts counselors here on earth to help us process tough situations. I thought that I could pray and fast and shout it all out but it does not work that way, so I've had to come to a greater realization. He will not let me continue with this pain because He really desires to see me whole. He wants me out of this self-imposed bondage and living the abundant life he speaks of in His word. I love Jesus!

€

To date the tests indicate the virus is not found and is undetected in my body. I believe and speak that I am healed. It is human nature to worry or be concerned about what others may think or if they will believe. I have been through these questions many times and have inquired of God about it. God said the only thing that matters is whether I believe.

If others don't believe, it will not stop me from receiving His promises to me. The only person that can stop me is me. If I stop believing then that's it. When I stop believing the promises of God and His purpose for my life, then neither the promise nor the purpose can be fulfilled. I can not let that happen, so no matter what people say, think or do, I'm going to trust in my God and His word. I will have all that He has promised me through His word, including the written and spoken words of God.

www.ingramcontent.com/pod-product-compliance
Lightning Source LLC
Chambersburg PA
CBHW051813040426
42446CB00007B/645